W9-BBZ-440

WILD WICKED WONDERFUL

TOP 10: DADS

By Virginia Loh-Hagan

◯ 45th Parallel Press

Published in the United States of America by Cherry Lake Publishing
Ann Arbor, Michigan
www.cherrylakepublishing.com

Content Adviser: Stephen Ditchkoff, Professor of Wildlife Ecology and Management, Auburn University, Alabama
Reading Adviser: Marla Conn MS, Ed., Literacy specialist, Read-Ability, Inc.
Book Designer: Melinda Millward

Photo Credits: ©SKapl/Thinkstock, cover, 1; ©Dennis Jacobsen/Shutterstock.com, 5; ©EastVillage Images/Shutterstock.com, 6; ©Ivanov Gleb/Shutterstock.com, 6; ©Dennis W. Donohue/Shutterstock.com, 6; ©Alta Oosthuizen/Shutterstock.com, 7; ©Nick Biemans/Shutterstock.com, 8; ©patrickkavanagh/http://www.flickr.com/CC-BY-2.0, 10; ©Auscape/Getty Images, 11; ©Photocech/Shutterstock.com, 12; ©belizar/Shutterstock.com, 12; ©aaxaoonxaa/iStockphoto, 13; ©Matthew Robinson/http://www.flickr.com/CC-BY-2.0, 14; ©Jupiterimages/Thinkstock, 14; ©Ryan Hodnett /http://www.flickr.com/CC BY-SA 2.0, 14; ©Mr. SUTTIPON YAKHAM/Shutterstock.com, 15; ©Tylinek/Shutterstock.com, 16; ©MarclSchauer/Shutterstock.com, 16; ©Hdcaputo/Dreamstime.com, 16; ©Rinus Baak/Dreamstime.com, 17; ©jack perks/Shutterstock.com, 18; ©blickwinkel/Alamy Stock Photo, 19; ©Rudmer Zwerver/Dreamstime.com, 20; ©Ute von Ludwiger/Shutterstock.com, 22; ©Jordi Prat Puig/Shutterstock.com, 22; ©Maniec/Dreamstime.com, 22; ©Belinda Wright/Getty Images, 23; ©Pug1979/Dreamstime.com, 24; ©Brad Wilson/DVM/Getty Images, 24; ©Michael & Patricia Fogden/Getty Images, 25; ©Vladimir Seliverstov/Dreamstime.com, 26; ©Stefan Christmann/BIA/Getty Images, 27; ©Anna Andych/Shutterstock.com, 28; ©Micalitus/Thinkstock, 28; ©Mariusz Niedzwiedzki/Shutterstock.com, 28; ©creativemarc/Shutterstock.com, 29; ©Dimijian Greg/Getty Images, 30; ©Chris Lorenz/Dreamstime.com, 31

Graphic Element Credits: ©tukkki/Shutterstock.com, back cover, front cover, multiple interior pages; ©paprika/Shutterstock.com, back cover, front cover, multiple interior pages; ©Silhouette Lover/Shutterstock Images, multiple interior pages

45th Parallel Press is an imprint of Cherry Lake Publishing.

Library of Congress Cataloging-in-Publication Data

Names: Loh-Hagan, Virginia, author.
Title: Top 10—Dads / by Virginia Loh-Hagan.
Other titles: Dads
Description: Ann Arbor : Cherry Lake Publishing, 2016. | Includes bibliographical references and index.
Identifiers: LCCN 2015050722| ISBN 9781634710985 (hardcover) | ISBN 9781634711975 (pdf) |
    ISBN 9781634712965 (pbk.) | ISBN 9781634713955 (ebook)
Subjects: LCSH: Parental behavior in animals—Juvenile literature.
Classification: LCC QL762 .L64 2016 | DDC 591.56/3—dc23
LC record available at https://lccn.loc.gov/2015050722

Printed in the United States of America
Corporate Graphics

About the Author

Dr. Virginia Loh-Hagan is an author, university professor, former classroom teacher, and curriculum designer. She dedicates this book to Bill, who was like a dad to her. She lives in San Diego with her very tall husband and very naughty dogs. To learn more about her, visit www.virginialoh.com.

TABLE OF CONTENTS

INTRODUCTION

Animals have babies. Babies ensure **survival** of the **species**. Survive means to live. Species means groups of animals. More babies mean more animals.

Baby animals are cute. But they're helpless. They're little. They don't have any skills. They're **prey**. Prey are hunted as food. They need help. They need moms. They need dads.

Animal dads are special. Some protect. Some care. Some teach. Some help animal moms. But some don't. Some don't help at all. Some are dangerous.

Some animal dads are extreme. Some of the most exciting dads are in the animal world!

Some animal babies are part of the food cycle. Dads protect them.

chapter one
LIONS

Lions live in Africa. They live in **prides**. A pride is a lion family. Each pride has one adult male. These dads rule their prides. Each dad mates with several females. Mate means to make babies. Dads can have many **cubs**. Cubs are babies.

Other male lions attack. They fight for control. They want to rule the pride. They kill other males' cubs. They only want their own cubs.

Lion dads have an important job. They protect their pride. They protect their cubs.

Male lions are deadly hunters.
They're fast. They're strong.

Lions' manes make them get hot. This tires them easily.

Some lion dads kick their sons out of the pride. Male cubs grow older. They become a threat. Lion dads fight them. They want control.

Lion dads fight hard. But they mostly sleep. They sleep 20 hours a day. They save energy to fight.

Lion moms do most of the work. They take care of cubs. They hunt. Lion dads babysit. They play rough. They have powerful jaws. But they're gentle when playing with cubs.

Cubs play with their dads' tails. They play with their **manes**. Manes are extra neck hair. Some lion dads like playing. Some snarl. Some bat the cubs away.

HUMANS DO WHAT?!?

Philippe Morgese is a single dad. He has a daughter named Emma. He puts barrettes in her hair. He does pigtails. Then, he does braids. He practices a lot. He teaches classes. He teaches hairstyling. He teaches brushing. He teaches how to make ponytails. He teaches how to make buns. He teaches braiding. He said, "It's not even about the hair. It's about the bond. It's about coming together and sharpening our skills. I'm excited to inspire." He started a Web page. It's called "Daddy Daughter Hair Factory." Dads post pictures. Morgese won a contest. Greg Wickherst started the contest. Wickherst is also a single dad. He went to beauty school. He learned to fix hair. He created a Web site. It's called "Dads Guide to Surviving Hair." He posts lessons, contests, and stories. Dads do anything for their daughters.

Chapter two

ANTECHINUSES

Antechinuses live in Australia. They're like special mice. They become adults at 11 months. The males live for three more weeks. They only live long enough to make babies.

Male antechinuses mate. They find females. They fight for females. Sometimes they lose. They find another female. They have to mate.

Making babies is their main job. They don't eat. They don't drink. They don't sleep. They save energy. They focus on mating.

Antechinuses mate in the winter.

Antechinuses mate for 12 hours. They get tired. Then they die. They give up their lives. They do this for their babies.

chapter three

GOLDEN JACKALS

Golden jackals live around the Middle East and India. They mate for life. Dads and moms stay together. They take care of babies together. Moms have babies in **burrows**. Burrows are holes in the ground. Dads help dig. Or they find dens. They make sure their families have homes.

Jackal babies need food. They eat every 2 hours. Jackal dads find food. They hunt. They **scavenge**. They eat dead animals.

They **regurgitate**. They throw up their food. They feed vomit to their babies. Jackal dads must live. Their babies

Jackal dads find moms by howling.

would die without them. Dads make sure their families have food.

Chapter four

GIANT WATER BUGS

Giant water bugs live in freshwater. Dads do pushups in the water. This creates waves. It draws moms to them. They mate. Moms climb on dads' backs. They lay eggs on dads' wings. They lay about 100 eggs. Then, moms leave.

Dads carry the eggs. They wait for eggs to hatch. They do this for 1 to 3 weeks. They collect water. They make sure the eggs don't dry out.

Dads can't fly. They can't swim. They have to protect the eggs. They have deadly bites. They have poison. They'll attack bigger animals. They attack fish, turtles, and snakes.

Giant water bugs can grow to 5 inches (12.7 centimeters).

They won't let their eggs get eaten.

chapter five

RHEAS

Rheas live in South America. They're large birds. They don't fly. Dads make loud booming noises. They wiggle their long necks. They attract moms. They mate with several moms.

Dads build a nest. Different moms lay eggs in one nest. Each nest can have 10 to 60 eggs. Moms leave.

Dads sit on the eggs. They do this for 6 weeks. They rarely leave the nest. They live on less food.

Baby rheas stay close to their dads. They do this for two

Rhea males mate with 2 to 12 females.

years. Dads take care of the babies. They protect. They guard. They attack. They fight. They won't let anything happen to their babies.

Chapter six

STICKLEBACK FISH

Stickleback fish live in the northern part of the world. They're extreme carpenters. Their kidneys make **spiggin**. Spiggin is special glue. They use this glue to build nests. They dig a small pit. They fill it with water plants and sand. They glue everything together. They make a tunnel. They do this by swimming quickly.

They find moms. They do a zigzag dance. They lure up to five moms. Moms swim through the tunnels. They lay eggs in the nests. Dads swim inside the nest. They chase

It takes 5 to 6 hours for stickleback fish to make a nest.

moms out. Then, they **fertilize** the eggs. Dads help the eggs turn into babies.

Stickleback fish dads become colorful when ready to mate.

There can be 40 to 300 eggs in the nest. Dads fan the eggs. They use their fins. They fan up to 400 beats per minute. They do this night and day. This gives eggs oxygen to breathe. This also washes away waste.

They protect the eggs. Many animals eat fish eggs. Dads chase them out.

The eggs hatch. Dads keep the babies together. Dads suck up runaway babies. Then they spit the runaways back into the nest. Dads do this for a few days. Then, the fish grow up. They leave the nest. The dads' job is done.

Did You Know...?

- Mammals are more like their dads. Dads pass on more genes.

- Only one in eight male lions survive to become adults.

- Golden jackals look like little wolves. Moms give off a powerful smell. Dads circle moms. They rub their sides. This is how they date. They have babies each year for about 8 years.

- Some people in Asia eat fried giant water bugs. They also use the dads' chemicals. They use it to make an expensive dipping sauce.

- Sea horse dads fight other dads. They fight for moms. They wrestle with their tails. They snap their heads at each other.

Chapter seven

JACANAS

Jacanas are waterbirds. They live in the tropics. They walk on water plants. They swim. They dive. Dads make nests. They use plants. They keep eggs dry and warm. They slide the eggs under their wings.

Moms lay about four eggs. They leave the dads. They look for new dads. Then, they mate. They have many partners.

Dads protect the eggs. They don't know if the eggs are theirs or not. It doesn't matter. They care for all the babies.

Jacana dads carry eggs under their wings if they have to move to new nests.

Chapter eight

DARWIN'S FROGS

Darwin's frogs live in forest streams. They live in Chile and Argentina. Moms lay about 40 eggs. Dads watch over the eggs. They do this for 3 to 4 weeks.

The eggs start to move. Dads eat the eggs. They keep the eggs in their **vocal sacs**. Vocal sacs are skin bags. They help frogs breathe. They help frogs make noise.

The eggs hatch inside dads. They become **tadpoles**. Tadpoles are baby frogs. They eat their own egg leftovers. They eat food inside their dads' vocal sacs.

Darwin's frogs play dead to fight off hunters.

Tadpoles grow for 6 weeks. Then dads throw up the babies. The babies hop out of their dad's mouth. They swim away.

Chapter nine

EMPEROR PENGUINS

Emperor penguins live in Antarctica. It's the coldest place on Earth. Emperor penguins make babies in the middle of winter.

Moms lay one egg. Then, they leave. They find fish. They're gone for 2 months.

Dads take care of eggs. Eggs can't touch the ground. They'd freeze to death. Dads make a nest with their feet. They balance eggs on their toes. They don't move. They don't eat. They do this for about 65 days. Dads huddle together. They keep warm.

Emperor penguin dads have a brood pouch, which is feathered skin. It protects eggs.

Moms return. They regurgitate food for chicks. Dads finally leave. They go find food.

chapter ten

SEA HORSES

Sea horses live in the tropics. Dads find moms. Dads change colors. They swim close to moms. They hold their tails. They spin. They dance. They do this for 3 days. Dancing makes dads look like they have big bellies. Moms love big bellies. Big bellies attract them.

Moms and dads dance close to each other. They do this for about 8 hours. Dads have pouches. They pump water through their pouches. This opens up the pouches. Moms lay eggs in these pouches. They lay hundreds of eggs. They can lay up to 1,500 eggs. Moms get skinnier. Dads get fatter.

Sea horse dads' pouches are open for about 6 seconds.

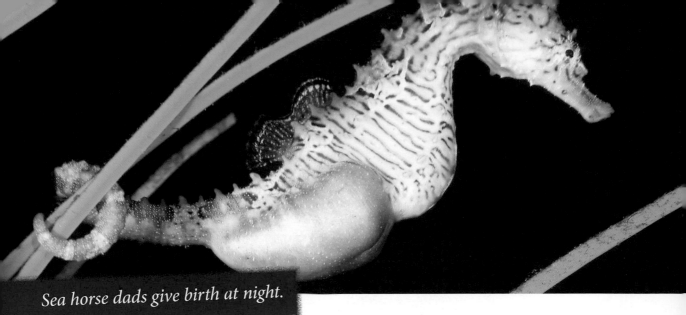

Sea horse dads give birth at night.

Eggs grow in the dads. Dads' pouches have special walls. The eggs stick to the walls. The walls provide food. The walls provide air. They keep the eggs safe.

Dads carry the eggs for 9 to 45 days. The eggs hatch inside the pouches. The water inside is salty. It prepares babies for ocean life.

Dads have **contractions**. Muscles push babies out. Baby sea horses swim away. They're fully grown. But they're small. Dads find another mom.

Sea horse dads help keep the species alive. Moms need a lot of energy to make eggs. Dads help by having the babies.

WHEN ANIMALS ATTACK!

Mockingbirds attacked people. They were angry birds! They did this in Houston, Texas. They dive-bombed. They poked with their beaks. They dug into people's backs. Eliana Crenshaw-Gibbs said, "I felt something hit my back. ...I turn around and see the bird coming at me, so I start running." The birds were protecting a nest. The nest had baby birds. The nest was in a tree. Cliff Shackelford works for the Texas Parks and Wildlife Department. He said, "The adult birds are merely being good parents. Such dive-bombing is quite a seasonal occurrence." People stayed away. They felt they were in a scary movie. The movie is *The Birds*. It's by Alfred Hitchcock.

CONSIDER THIS!

TAKE A POSITION! The animal kingdom is complex. Animal dads are extreme. Some kill their own babies. Why do they do this? Do you think this is right? Argue your point with reasons and evidence.

SAY WHAT? Read *Extreme Moms*. This is another 45th Parallel Press book by Virginia Loh-Hagan. Compare the moms to the dads in this book. Explain how they are similar. Explain how they are different.

THINK ABOUT IT! Humans share behaviors with animals. In what ways do human dads behave like animal dads?

LEARN MORE!
- Berger, Melvin, and Gilda Berger. *101 Animal Babies*. New York: Scholastic, 2013.
- Collard, Sneed B., III, and Steve Jenkins (illustrator). *Animal Dads*. Boston: Houghton Mifflin, 1997.

GLOSSARY

burrows (BUR-ohz) underground holes or tunnels

contractions (kuhn-TRAK-shuhnz) muscle movements pushing out babies

cubs (KUHBZ) baby animals like cats or bears

fertilize (FUR-tuh-lize) to help eggs turn into babies

manes (MAYNZ) lions' neck hair

mates (MAYTS) makes babies

prey (PRAY) animals that are hunted for food

prides (PRYDZ) groups of lions

regurgitate (rih-GUR-ji-tate) to eat food and throw it back up

scavenge (SKAV-uhnj) to eat dead animals

species (SPEE-sheez) groups of animals

spiggin (SPIG-in) special glue that stickleback fish make

survival (sur-VYE-vuhl) the act of staying alive

tadpoles (TAD-pohlz) baby frogs or toads

vocal sacs (VOH-kuhl SAKS) skin bags of frogs that help them breathe and make noise

INDEX